IELTS READING STRATEGIES

The Ultimate Guide With Tips And Tricks On How To Get A Target Band Score Of 8.0+ In 10 Minutes A Day

RACHEL MITCHELL

Copyright © 2017

All rights reserved.

ISBN: 9781973427582

TEXT COPYRIGHT © [RACHEL MITCHELL]

all rights reserved. No part of this guide may be reproduced in any form without permission in writing from the publisher except in the case of brief quotations embodied in critical articles or reviews.

Legal & disclaimer

The information contained in this book and its contents is not designed to replace or take the place of any form of medical or professional advice; and is not meant to replace the need for independent medical, financial, legal or other professional advice or services, as may be required. The content and information in this book have been provided for educational and entertainment purposes only.

The content and information contained in this book have been compiled from sources deemed reliable, and it is accurate to the best of the author's knowledge, information, and belief. However, the author cannot guarantee its accuracy and validity and cannot be held liable for any errors and/or omissions. Further, changes are periodically made to this book as and when needed. Where appropriate and/or necessary, you must consult a professional (including but not limited to your doctor, attorney, financial advisor or such other professional advisor) before using any of the suggested remedies, techniques, or information in this book.

Upon using the contents and information contained in this book, you agree to hold harmless the author from and against any damages, costs, and expenses, including any legal fees potentially resulting from the application of any of the information provided by this book. This disclaimer applies to any loss, damages or injury caused by the use and application, whether directly or indirectly, of any advice or information presented, whether for breach of contract, tort, negligence, personal injury, criminal intent, or under any other cause of action.

You agree to accept all risks of using the information presented inside this book.

You agree that by continuing to read this book, where appropriate and/or necessary, you shall consult a professional (including but not limited to your doctor, attorney, or financial advisor or such other advisor as needed) before using any of the suggested remedies, techniques, or information in this book.

TABLE OF CONTENT

INTRODUCTION 6
IELTS READING TEST INTRODUCTION 7
IELTS READING MARKING AND ASSESSMENT 8
PRIMARY SKILLS NEEDED 9
IELTS READING QUESTION TYPES 10

- Matching Headings: 10
- Matching Information to Paragraphs: 12
- Multiple-Choice Questions: 15
- Summary Completion: 17
- Completion Tasks: 21
- Note Completion: 23
- Table Completion: 24
- Sentence Completion: 25
- Flow-Chart Completion: 26
- Classification Type: 27
- Matching Sentence Endings: 29
- Yes, No, Not Given Questions: 31
- True, False, Not Given Questions: 33
- Short Answer Questions: 35

TIPS TO IMPROVE YOUR READING SKILL 37
IELTS READING STRATEGIES 38

THE LIST OF WORDS AND PHRASES USED IN THE IELTS READING EXAM THAT HAVE THE SIMILAR MEANING 41

- SYNONYMS/A 41
- SYNONYMS/B 47
- SYNONYMS/C 50
- SYNONYMS/D 57
- SYNONYMS/E 62
- SYNONYMS/F 65
- SYNONYMS/G 68
- SYNONYMS/H 70
- SYNONYMS/K 76
- SYNONYMS/L 77
- SYNONYMS/M 79
- SYNONYMS/N 82
- SYNONYMS/O 84
- SYNONYMS/P 86
- SYNONYMS/Q 90
- SYNONYMS/R 91
- SYNONYMS/S 95
- SYNONYMS/T 100
- SYNONYMS/U 103
- SYNONYMS/V 105
- SYNONYMS/W 106

CONCLUSION 108

CHECK OUT OTHER BOOKS **109**

INTRODUCTION

Thank you and congratulate you for downloading the book *"IELTS Reading Strategies: The Ultimate Guide with Tips and Tricks on How to Get a Target Band Score of 8.0+ in 10 Minutes a Day."*

This book is well designed and written by an experienced native teacher from the USA who has been teaching IELTS for over 10 years. She really is the expert in training IELTS for students at each level. In this book, she will provide you all proven Formulas, Tips, Tricks, Strategies, Explanations, Structures, Reading Language, and Synonyms to help you easily achieve an 8.0+ in the IELTS Reading, even if your reading is not excellent. This book will also walk you through step-by-step on how to develop your reading skill; clearly analyze and explain the different types of questions that are asked for the IELTS Reading Test; provide you step-by-step instructions on how to answer each type of question excellently.

As the author of this book, Rachel Mitchell believes that this book will be an indispensable reference and trusted guide for you who may want to maximize your band score in IELTS Reading. Once you read this book, I guarantee you that you will have learned an extraordinarily wide range of useful, and practical IELTS Reading strategies, tips and tricks that will help you become a successful IELTS taker as well as you will even become a successful English user in work and in life within a short period of time only.

Take action today and start getting 8.0 + in IELTS Reading tomorrow!

Thank you again for purchasing this book, and I hope you enjoy it.

IELTS READING TEST INTRODUCTION

- The reading test **comes after the listening test**. It is the second section of the IELTS test.

- The reading test lasts **60 minutes** (do not get a break).

- There are **3 sections** (each section has 13 or 14 questions)

- There are **40 questions** in total.

- **No extra time is given** to transfer your answers from the questions to the answer sheet. Therefore, you have to complete the answer sheet within the 60 minutes.

- You must **use a pencil** to write answers on the Answer Sheet because it is scanned by a computer. That's the same as the IELTS listening test.

- There is **a wide variety of tasks** candidates may have to complete.

IELTS READING MARKING AND ASSESSMENT

- The scores are calculated by the number of correct answers you have. There are **40 questions** which are equivalent to **40 points**. Each time you get a correct answer, you get 1 point (no 1/2 points). That is how your band scores are calculated.
- You have to **follow the Instructions exactly** (e.g. must stay within word/number limit).
- **Spelling and grammar must be correct** *(e.g. singular or plural; use the correct form of the words)*. You will lose marks if you misspell a word or if you put a word in the wrong grammatical form.
- There is no deduction for a wrong answer - so if you're not sure, guess!
- **IELTS reading scores**

    According to official IELTS guidelines:

    Band 5.5 = 20 – 22 correct answers.

    Band 6.0 = 23 – 26 correct answers.

    Band 6.5 = 27 – 29 correct answers.

    Band 7.0 = 30 – 32 correct answers.

    Band 7.5 = 33 – 34 correct answers.

    Band 8.0 = 35 – 37 correct answers.

    Band 8.5 = 38 – 39 correct answers.

PRIMARY SKILLS NEEDED

- Searching and underlining key words.

- Looking for synonyms and parallel expressions.

- Skimming (reading the text very quickly).

- Scanning (looking for something without reading).

- Reading for specific information.

IELTS READING QUESTION TYPES

Matching Headings: you are asked to select headings of paragraphs and match them to the relevant paragraphs from a text. Matching headings is often one of the most difficult question types for Students. **Why?** The main reason is that the headings are usually very similar to each other. Also, you have more headings than you need for the question.

Questions 1 – 5

Sample Passage 6 has six sections, **A-F**.

Choose the correct heading for sections **A-D** and **F** from the list of headings below.

Write the correct number *i-ix* in boxes 1-5 on your answer sheet.

List of Headings

- i   The probable effects of the new international trade agreement
- ii The environmental impact of modern farming
- iii Farming and soil erosion
- iv The effects of government policy in rich countries
- v   Governments and management of the environment
- vi The effects of government policy in poor countries
- vii Farming and food output
- viii The effects of government policy on food output
- ix The new prospects for world trade

1	Section **A**
2	Section **B**
3	Section **C**
4	Section **D**

Example	Section **E**	vi

5	Section **F**

Matching Headings Tips:

1. Do this type of question first if it is on the test. By doing this, you will have a chance to get the general meaning of the text as a whole. This

will help you with the rest of the questions that require you to take a more detailed look at the text.

2. Check how many questions you need to answer.

3. Do not use any answer more than once.

4. Do not need to read the whole text.

5. Read the headings first and think about the topic of the text. Then, read the first, second and last sentences of the paragraph to understand the general meaning of the paragraph.

6. Identify and underline keywords within each heading

7. Try to look for synonyms or other words that have a similar meaning to words or phrases in the headings so you can rule out the correct answer.

Matching Information to Paragraphs: you will be asked to match statements in a list to corresponding paragraphs in the reading text. The match information task has been designed to test your ability to find specific information in the passage of text. In other words, this task focuses on your ability to locate specific information. You might be asked to find specific details, for example, a reason, a description, a comparison, a summary, a fact, or an explanation.

Questions 14 – 19

Sample Passage 7 has eight paragraphs labelled **A-H**.

Which paragraphs contains the following information?

*Write the correct letter **A-H** in boxes 14-19 on your answer sheet.*
NB   You may use any letter more than once.

14   a comparison of past and present transportation methods

15   how driving habits contribute to road problems

16   the relative merits of cars and public transport

17   the writer's prediction on future solutions

18   the increasing use of motor vehicles

19   the impact of the car on city development

Questions 1-6

This reading passage has eight paragraphs, A-H.
Which paragraph contains the following information?

1. An explanation of how adjustments are made when navigating
2. Recent news about how navigation systems work
3. A comparison of tracking abilities
4. A study showing that scent and sound are not important
5. Explaining the importance of counting
6. A description of how ants navigate

Matching Information Tips:

1. Do this type of question last. You will be able to look for the correct information and the right answers more quickly and easily if you do other questions first since you were familiar with the passage.

2. Read the title of the passage.

3. Read the instructions carefully.

4. Look for and underline keywords, and highlight the kinds of information you need to find for each statement given such as a definition, a number, a name, an example or a description.

5. Use paraphrasing skill to look for words that have similar meaning. Take notes for synonym or antonyms. This will help you identify the correct answer.

6. All paragraphs contain an answer and some paragraphs contain more than one answer. Therefore, you may use any letter more than once. That means you might find the answer to different questions in the same paragraph.

7. The questions are not in the same order as the information in the passage.

Multiple-Choice Questions:

one question is given to you followed by four or five choices in which you have to choose the best one which will fit your answer.

Questions 10 – 12

*Choose the appropriate letters **A**, **B**, **C** or **D**.*

Write your answers in boxes 10-12 on your answer sheet.

10   Research completed in 1982 found that in the United States soil erosion

   A   reduced the productivity of farmland by 20 per cent.
   B   was almost as severe as in India and China.
   C   was causing significant damage to 20 per cent of farmland.
   D   could be reduced by converting cultivated land to meadow or forest.

11   By the mid-1980s, farmers in Denmark

   A   used 50 per cent less fertiliser than Dutch farmers.
   B   used twice as much fertiliser as they had in 1960.
   C   applied fertiliser much more frequently than in 1960.
   D   more than doubled the amount of pesticide they used in just 3 years.

12   Which one of the following increased in New Zealand after 1984?

   A   farm incomes
   B   use of fertiliser
   C   over-stocking
   D   farm diversification

Multiple-Choice Tips:

1. Read the instructions carefully, skim all the questions briefly to get an idea of the topics for which you will be searching when reading the text.

2. Try to predict the right answer before you read the text.

3. In multiple choice questions, remember to use the keywords in the question to help you find the right part of the text. Read that part again and consider all the options one by one.

4. Match the keywords in the question to their associated paragraph in the text. You need to know where to read to find the correct answer.

5. Locate the particular section of the paragraph in which the important information is located to find the answer.

6. You don't need to read the entire text from beginning to end because the questions follow the same order as the paragraphs.

7. The keyword you see in the question may not be written exactly the same as it is in the paragraph.

8. Only read the particular section of the paragraph which directly relates back to the question after you match the keyword or the synonym from the question to the corresponding paragraph.

Summary Completion: you will be given a summary of information from the text and there will be some gaps in that summary. You will either be given a list of words to fill the gaps with or asked to find the answers in the reading text. Your job is to insert some of the words from the list into the gaps; or if you are asked to fill the gaps with words from the text, there will be more words in the list that are required to fill the gaps. All of the information contained in the summary will also be contained in the reading text but they will use **synonyms** and **paraphrasing**. Therefore, don't expect to see the same words. The summary may relate to the whole passage or only a part of it and the text of the summary will follow the order of the text of the passage.

SUMMARY COMPLETION

Questions 1-6
Complete the summary below.
Choose *no more than two words* from the passage for each answer.

The Main Functions of the Police

The police are persons empowered to enforce the law, protect property and reduce 1...................... Their powers include the 2..................... use of force. The term is most commonly associated with police services of a state that are authorized to exercise the police power of that state within a defined legal or 3..................... area of responsibility. Police forces are often defined as organizations separate from any 4....................., or other organizations involved in the 5..................... of the state against 6..................... .

In other Summary Completion exercises in the IELTS Reading Test, candidates are required to choose words from a box in order to complete the task. There will be more words than spaces and they are usually different words from the ones in the passage. This tests a candidate's ability to recognise synonyms and paraphrase.

Complete the summary below.

Choose **ONE WORD ONLY** from the passage for each answer.

Write your answers in boxes 24–26 on your answer sheet.

How children acquire a sense of identity

First, children come to realise that they can have an effect on the world around them, for example by handling objects, or causing the image to move when they face a **24** .... This aspect of self-awareness is difficult to research directly, because of **25** .... problems.

Secondly, children start to become aware of how they are viewed by others. One important stage in this process is the visual recognition of themselves which usually occurs when they reach the age of two. In Western societies at least, the development of self awareness is often linked to a sense of **26** .... , and can lead to disputes.

Questions 18–22

Complete the summary using the list of words, A–I, below.

Write the correct letter, A–I, in boxes 18–22 on your answer sheet.

Weather during the Little Ice Age

Documentation of past weather conditions is limited: our main sources of knowledge of conditions in the distant past are 18 .... and 19 .... We can deduce that the Little Ice Age was a time of 20 .... , rather than of consistent freezing. Within it there were some periods of very cold winters, others of 21 .... and heavy rain, and yet others that saw 22 .... with no rain at all.

A climatic shifts	B ice cores	C tree rings
D glaciers	E interactions	F weather observations
G heat waves	H storms	I written accounts

Summary Completion Tips:

1. Read the instructions to the questions very carefully.

2. Skim through the summary. Ignoring the blanks to understand its general meaning.

3. Predict the right answers before looking at the options.

4. Don't waste time looking at parts of the passage that are not included in the summary.

5. You need to focus on keywords before and after the blank.

6. Check with the passage. You can use your keyword strategy to identify the correct part of the passage but remember you are looking for synonyms.

7. Check to see if your word is grammatical. Think about nouns, adjectives, verbs, and adverbs.

8. The answers are mostly in order. Sometimes they'll all be in order; but once in a while, there will be an answer that comes before another answer. However, don't worry about this because the keywords are specific and easy to find.

Completion Tasks:

These tasks are note completion, flowchart completion, sentence completion, table completion, and summary completion tasks.

Completion Tasks Tips:

Here are some basic tips that you need to learn to deal with this type of question excellently:

1. There will be a words limit, so please read the instructions carefully and see the words limit that you need to write in order to fill in the gaps. There will be usually *NO MORE THAN ONE WORDS, TWO WORDS* or *THREE WORDS*, so underline this and remember while you fill in the exercise.

2. Secondly, usually for most tasks in IELTS reading, the questions in the tasks and the gaps are followed in the same order as they will appear in the text. However, please remember and keep in mind that when you see a completion task, the questions and the gaps will not necessarily follow the order that they will be shown in the text.

3. You should copy the words that you find in the text exactly the same way in order to fill in the gaps. Hence, they have to both fit grammatically and syntactically.

4. Try to predict what kind of words are missing, for example, a noun, a verb, an adjective or an adverb. The words before and after the gap help you understand what is missing.

5. You should underline key words that precede gaps. These keywords are going to guide you through the text in order to find where the correct answer is located. You should be careful of paraphrasing.

6. In IELTS, you should always concentrate on meanings, not on words. That is always helpful to be good at skimming and scanning techniques.

Note Completion:

*Choose **NO MORE THAN ONE WORD AND/OR A NUMBER** from the passage.*

Blombos Cave discovery

Background
- location: South Africa
- the date digging began: 1 ....

- Previous ancient objects found in this area
  - 2 ....
  - 3 ....
  - 4 ....

Recent findings
- a mixture containing a substance called 5 .... (used to provide colour)
- equipment
- a range of additional 6 .... including animal bone and charcoal

Conclusion
- in prehistoric times, humans knew basic 7 ....

Table Completion:

Questions 29-35

*Complete the table below using information from Reading Passage 3. Write **NO MORE THAN THREE WORDS** for each answer. Write your answers in boxes 29-35 on your answer sheet.*

PERIOD	STYLE OF PERIOD	BUILDING MATERIALS	CHARACTERISTICS
Before 18th century	*Example* traditional	... (29) ...	
1920s	introduction of ... (30) ...	steel, glass and concrete	exploration of latest technology
1930s - 1950s	... (31) ...		geometric forms
1960s	decline of Modernism	pre-fabricated sections	... (32) ...
1970s	end of Modernist era	traditional materials	... (33) ... of historic buildings
1970s	beginning of ... (34) ... era	metal and glass	sophisticated techniques paraded
1980s	Post-Modernism		... (35) ...

Sentence Completion:

Example Question

Questions 38 – 40

Complete the sentences below.

*Choose **NO MORE THAN TWO WORDS** from the text for each answer.*

Write your answers in boxes 38-40 on your answer sheet.

38   Von Frisch discovered the difference between dance types by changing the position of the ....

39   The dance outside the hive points in the direction of the ....

40   The angle of the dance from the vertical shows the angle of the food from the ....

Flow-Chart Completion:

Question 33-40

Complete the flow-chart below.
Choose **NO MORE THAN THREE WORDS** from the text for each answer.
Write your answers in boxes 33-40 on your answer sheet.

The Production Process

⬇

The newspaper is compiled at the editorial headquarters by the journalists.

⬇

The final version of the text is 33 .... to the printing centre.

⬇

The pages arrive by facsimile.

⬇

The pages are converted into 34 ....

⬇

35 .... are made for use in the printing presses.

⬇

The LGVs are 36 .... by computer.

⬇

The LGVs collect the reels of paper.

⬇

The LGVs remove the 37 .... from the reel.

⬇

The reel is 38 ....

⬇

The reel is trimmed and prepared by the 39 ....

⬇

The reel is taken to the press.   The reel is taken to the 40 ....

Classification Type: you need to classify the information you read in the passage. In other words, you need to sort statements or features into different categories. There are always 3 categories and these categories are of the same type. You are also given several numbered statements or features. Each category is given a letter. So on your answer sheet, you need to write a letter, A, B, or C.

Questions 1-9

Classify the following statements as referring to

- **A** Charlie Moore
- **B** Lewis Williams
- **C** Emily Cope

Write the appropriate letters **A, B** or **C** in boxes 1-9 on your answer sheet.

1) British people don't appreciate art because they don't see enough art around them all the time.

2) British museums aim to appeal to popular tastes in art.

3) The average Englishman likes the works of Turner and Constable.

4) Britain, like every other country, has its own view of what art is.

5) In Britain, interest in art is mainly limited to traditional forms such as representational painting.

6) British art has always been affected by other cultures.

7) Galleries in other countries are of better quality that those in Britain.

8) People are not raised to appreciate art.

9) The British have a limited knowledge of art.

Classification Tips:

1. Always be sure to read the instructions first.

2. Skim the reading text to get its general meaning.

3. Search for and underline the **"keywords"** in the statements. Usually, some of words in the questions have the same meaning to words in the passage. You will probably find the answer if you find the similar words.

4. It is important to note that, in classification tasks, the questions will not be in the same order as you read them in the passage. Therefore, it's a good idea to circle information that you'll need later.

5. Some letters, or categories may be used more than once while some letters may not be used at all.

6. Always give an answer even if you are unsure. You won't lose marks if the answer is wrong and you may just get it right.

Matching Sentence Endings:

you are going to be given a list of incomplete sentences and another list with possible endings. Your job is to choose the correct ending for each sentence based on the reading text. This means you will have to choose their ending correctly based on a number of options. All options are going to have similar meanings, so this is what makes this task rather challenging. However, the good news is that the sentences in the task will appear in the order that they will appear in the text; so you will know where to find each piece of information that each sentence conveys while you scan through the text.

Complete each sentence with the correct ending A-J from the box below. Write only the letter. You do not need to use all of the sentence endings.

1. Strawberries may help to choose one
2. In non-human tests fisetin was shown choose one
3. Specialists believe choose one
4. Fisetin has choose one
5. Mahar wants to soon begin choose one
6. Alzheimer's is choose one
7. Almost a quarter of the world's population is predicted choose one
8. A reduction in the number of cases of cognitive diseases suffered by the elderly will reduce choose one

A. to be over the age of 60 by the year 2050.
B. may be described as a new superfood.
C. to reduce swelling of an organ.
D. an increasing problem around the world.
E. been studied for over 10 years.
F. more testing should be carried out to find out the benefits of fisetin.
G. the predicted burden on health services in the future.
H. cure diseases suffered by the elderly.
I. controlled testing of fisetin on people.
J. are highly toxic.

Matching Sentence Tips:

1. Read the sentences and underline keywords. Especially those phrases that are hard to be paraphrased. These underlined words and phrases will help you and guide you to find the answer in the text through scanning.

2. When highlighting keywords, it is often a good idea to highlight any names including place names or dates. These are often easy to find in the reading text.

3. Read the incomplete sentences first and try to predict how each sentence will end before you look at the endings or the text.

4. Go to the text and scan the text in order to locate where this piece of information that the sentence states.

5. Read the piece of information that you found in the text. It may be a whole paragraph, so you need to read this piece of information carefully and then choose the right option.

6. Make sure that the option that you have chosen fits the first half of the sentence not only in grammar and syntax but also in the meaning that the sentence tries to express.

7. The answers are in the same order in a text as they are in the questions.

Yes, No, Not Given Questions: the **YES, NO, NOT GIVEN** questions are all about the writer's opinion. It's not about the facts but about what the writer thinks. If the answer is **YES**, it means that the statement in the question agrees with the claims of the writer. If the answer is **NO**, it means the statement is opposite; it contradicts the claims of the writer. **NOT GIVEN** means it is impossible to say what the writer thinks about.

Questions 32–35

Do the following statements agree with the claims of the writer in Reading Passage 3?

In boxes 32–35 on your answer sheet, write

    YES   if the statement agrees with the claims of the writer
    NO   if the statement contradicts the claims of the writer
    NOT GIVEN   if it is impossible to say what the writer thinks about this

32   Helium chooses to be on its own.

33   Helium is a very cold substance.

34   High-tech industries in Asia use more helium than laboratories and manufacturers in other parts of the world.

35   The US Congress understood the possible consequences of the HPA.

Yes, No, Not Given Tips:

1. Ignore anything you already know about the topic and don't make assumptions. Based your answers on the text only.

2. Identify any words that qualify the statement. For example, *some, all, mainly, often, always* and *occasionally*. These words are there to test

if you have read the whole statement because they can change the meaning. Be careful.

3. When you see verbs that qualify statements such as ***know, suggest, claim, and believe***. For example, *"the woman claimed she was a doctor"* and *"the women is a doctor"* mean they are different.

4. Don't skim and scan the text. To find the correct answer, you will have to read the appropriate part of the text very carefully in order to understand what the writer means.

5. Don't look for words that exactly match those in the statements. Instead, you should look for synonyms.

6. If you can't find the information you are looking for, then it is probably **NOT GIVEN**. Don't waste time looking for something that is not there.

7. Answers are in the same order they appear in the text. Do not waste time going back.

True, False, Not Given Questions: you will be given a number of factual statements and you have to check in the text if they are true, false or not given. The **TRUE, FALSE, NOT GIVEN** questions are all about factual information in the passage. It's not about opinions; it's about **fact**. **TRUE** means that the statement in the question agrees with the information in the passage. **FALSE** means the statement in the question contradicts the information in the Passage *("contradicts" means it's the opposite meaning)*. **NOT GIVEN** means there is no information on this. This task is used to assess the candidate's ability to find the particular information found in the passage.

Questions 1 – 8

Do the following statements agree with the information given in the text?

In boxes 1-8 on your answer sheet, write

    TRUE   if the statement agrees with the information
    FALSE   if the statement contradicts the information
    NOT GIVEN if there is no information on this

1. You should not arrive more than half an hour before your allocated starting time.
2. Your Rider Identity Card will be sent to you before the event.
3. Some roads may have normal traffic flow on them.
4. Helmets are compulsory for all participants.
5. Refreshments are free to all participants during the ride.
6. If you need a rest you must get off the road.
7. First aid staff can provide cycle capes.
8. Bike Events will charge you for the return of your bike.

True, False, Not Given Tips:

1. Read the instructions carefully and make sure you know if it is a **true/ false/ not given** question.

2. Read all the statements carefully. Trying to understand what the whole sentence means rather than simply highlighting keywords.

3. You need to find the right part of the text before you can answer the question. Remember that the questions follow the text.

4. Finding key ideas in the text.

5. Look for **expressions of uncertainty**. Look for modal verbs like *could, might,* or *must*. Look for expressions which indicate <u>uncertainty</u>, such as *suggest, think, claim, believe,* and *know.* For example, *it is thought that* or *many scientists believe that.*

6. If you can't find the answer or if you are really unsure, mark it as **NOT GIVEN** and move on to the next question.

7. If the question in the reading test is **TRUE, FALSE, NOT GIVEN**, you must remember to write **TRUE** or **FALSE** or **NOT GIVEN** on your answer sheet; you **can't** write YES or NO. That means if the answer is **TRUE** and you write **YES**, the answer will be marked wrong.

8. You can write **a letter** instead of **a word** for your answer. That means if your answer is **TRUE,** you can write only **T**. It still means true and IELTS will give you a correct answer for that one point.

Short Answer Questions: where you have to give a very short answer with a maximum of three words or a number. Here is a sample question.

Answer the questions below.

*Choose **NO MORE THAN THREE WORDS AND/OR A NUMBER** from the passage for each answer.*

Write your answers in boxes 18-20 on your answer sheet.

18 What is the life expectancy of Earth?
19 What kind of signals from other intelligent civilisations are SETI scientists searching for?
20 How many stars are the world's most powerful radio telescopes searching?

Answer the questions below.

*Choose **NO MORE THAN TWO WORDS** from the passage for each answer.*

Write your answers in boxes 8-13 on your answer sheet.

8   Before Perkin's discovery, with what group in society was the colour purple associated?
9   What potential did Perkin immediately understand that his new dye had?
10 What was the name finally used to refer to the first colour Perkin invented?
11 What was the name of the person Perkin consulted before setting up his own dye works?

Short Answer Questions Tips:

1. You don't have to read every word of the text. The questions test your ability to skim and scan for specific information, so you won't have time to read every word.

2. The answers appear in the same order of the text.

3. Skim and scan the passage quickly and understand the overall meaning.

4. Look at and understand the questions first before you start reading the text.

5. Make sure you don't go over the word limit as stated above the answers.

6. Don't give your opinion, just the answer in the text.

7. Read the instructions carefully and note the word limit.

8. Read and understand the questions. Think about the information you will need to find.

9. Underline any keywords in the questions. Think about synonyms or paraphrases for these keywords.

10. Read the section containing the answer carefully and identify the right answer.

TIPS TO IMPROVE YOUR READING SKILL

1. Reading a lot (no shortcut). You will only be able to improve your reading skill with time and practice. Doing more reading about subjects that you are interested in.

2. Reading a lot of IELTS passages in the Cambridge books.

3. Analyzing each passage carefully, finding the 'keywords', understanding each passage, and finding the correct answer to each question.

4. Analyzing your mistakes and the correct answers.

IELTS READING STRATEGIES

Here is a list of IELTS reading strategies:

1. Because the time for IELTS reading test is limited, you don't spend too much time reading the whole text. Do not read word for word everything you see. You don't have to understand everything.

2. Just go straight to read the questions first, and then read the passage.

3. Use skills such as skimming and scanning to quickly read for the main idea or look for keywords or look for specific detail like numbers, names or dates.

4. There are three passages in the IELTS test. The first passage is the easiest, then the second passage and then the third passage. Since the first passage is easier, it's a good idea to spend less time on this one.

5. Don't waste time on difficult questions. Do easier sections first, and do difficult sections later.

6. Read all instructions carefully. Especially for questions which require you to answer in *NO MORE THAN THREE WORDS OR A NUMBER*.

7. Most of the answers to questions are in the correct order in the passage, so you don't need to go back to the beginning to find the next answer.

8. Search for and underline the **"keywords"**. Usually, some of words in the questions have the same meaning to words in the passage. For example, if the passage includes the words *"towns and cities"*, *"elderly people"*, the question might use the words *"urban"*, *"senior citizens"*.

Therefore, you will probably find the answer if you find the similar words.

9. Circling transitional words and phrases when you look for details such as *"in contrast"*, *"however"* in order to ensure that these words and phrases **work as a sign** that important information may appear before or after them.

10. Predict the correct answer.

11. Find the right part of the passage quickly. Read that part carefully. Read the sentences before and after the keywords that you have found to look for the correct answer.

12. IELTS is very big on paraphrasing and using a range of different language for the same meaning. Therefore, when you look at questions or statements, you do need to think about possible paraphrases. That will help you identify where the answer is and to actually get the right answer.

13. Common traps: one of the common traps you need to know is **COMPARISONS**. If you see a comparative sentence in the question *"more or less than"*, make sure you also find a comparison in the passage to find the correct answer.

14. Also look for these types of words: if they say *"all"* and the question says *"some"*, that's not a match. Likewise, if they say *"the majority"* and the question says *"some"*, that's also not a match. This is really testing your ability to understand the exact difference and the exact meaning of words.

15. Don't **"over-think"** the answer. Many students get the wrong answer simply because they think too hard about small differences in meaning.

16. Time management: you will have **60 minutes** for the reading test with **40 questions** in total. Therefore, you need to manage your time wisely.

17. Transfer your answers from the question sheet to your answer sheet carefully. When you transfer your answers to the answer sheet, don't get your answers mixed up spelling and grammar or you will lose points here. Don't be in a hurry. Be careful to check and double-check. If your writing is unclear, your answer will be marked wrong.

THE LIST OF WORDS AND PHRASES USED IN THE IELTS READING EXAM THAT HAVE THE SIMILAR MEANING

SYNONYMS/A

- annual = yearly = per year

- a rise = an increase = a growth.

- a decrease = a fall = a drop = a decline = a reduction

- already = not new

- a pair of = two

- allow = enable

- avoid = keep safe from

- all = every

- a great deal of = a lot of

- according to = depending on

- areas = parts

- affect = impact

- anticipate = foreshadow

- aid = help

- audience = viewer
- abnormal = unusual
- actor = performer
- attack = assault
- appearance = physiognomy
- amusing = funny = humorous
- aspects of life = existence
- alone = solely
- anxiety = fear
- assist their learning = improve their learning efficiency
- a considerable amount = a great deal = a lot
- a strong connection = a very close relationship
- assistant = apprentice
- autumn (British English) = fall (American English)
- abandoned = derelict
- a prevailing wind = against the wind
- average = normal
- animals = livestock

- accidentally = only by chance

- agencies = jurisdictions

- a (wide) variety of = a range of

- accept = tolerate

- actively notice = pay attention to

- a sense of duty = moral obligation

- ancient creatures = fossils

- a global team = an international working party

- at risk = vulnerable

- auditory problems = hearing loss

- achievement = success

- a psychological illness = a mental disorder

- affect = influence

- aggressive behavior = frustration and anger

- average-sized = medium-sized

- agree on = concur on

- alter = change

- a century = 100 years

- associated with = relationship
- achievement = attainment
- admit = acknowledge
- attempt = effort
- affect the environment = ruin the environment.
- a sharp decrease = a crash = a sudden serious fall in the price or value of something
- allow = grant permission
- aggressive = assertive = pushy
- aid = help = assist
- at the same time = at a time
- a few = a handful of
- achievable = realistic
- associated with = closely related to
- a similar way to = like
- ambitious = aspiring
- antagonize = provoke = embitter
- after = following = next

- afraid = frightened = scared

- always = forever

- apparent = obvious = evident

- accompanied by = together with

- ability = skill = aptitude

- accurate = correct = right

- awful = dreadful

- awkward = clumsy = uncoordinated

- approve = accept = ratify = endorse

- arrive = reach = come

- above = overhead

- allow = permit

- achieve = accomplish = attain

- artificial = fake = synthetic = false

- amazing = fantastic = astonishing = extraordinary = incredible = fabulous = wonderful

- angry = mad = furious

- active = energetic = animated = lively

- adequate = sufficient = enough = ample

- ask = question = inquire

- adjourn = postpone = recess

- active = energetic

- answer = reply = respond

- ask = question = request = inquire = query = examine.

- adult = grown-up

- average = ordinary = fair

- attraction = spectacular

- advocate = support = recommend

- arrogant = haughty

- after = behind

- awful = dreadful = terrible = bad = unpleasant

SYNONYMS/B

- businesses = companies

- beneath = under

- brief = short = concise

- broad = wide = expansive

- beautiful = gorgeous = graceful = elegant = pretty = lovely = attractive

- begin = start = open = initiate = commence

- based on = modelled on

- brave = courageous = fearless

- by = via

- busy = occupied

- build = construct

- big = enormous = huge = gigantic = vast = large = great.

- bright = intelligent = knowing = quick-witted = smart = shining = shiny = brilliant

- buy = purchase

- best = finest

- blend = combine = mix

- be put together = be composed

- be allowed = be entitled

- beautiful (view) = breathtaking = wonderful = picturesque

- beautiful (person) = attractive = gorgeous = good-looking.

- base = foundation

- brave = courageous

- be predicted to = be expected to

- be impossible = cannot

- building = construction

- before = prior

- because = since

- be given priority = preferential

- believe = trust = accept

- be successful = to prosper = be fortunate

- barren = unproductive = infertile

- below = under = lower

- beneficial = helpful = useful = advantageous

- become troublesome = interfere with

- before = prior to

- brain = mind

- be able = be capable = be qualified

- ban = prohibit = forbid

- before = prior = earlier

- beginning = start = initiate

- be raised = be lifted

- become aware of = realize

- boundaries = frontiers

- body language = gestures

- beautiful = pretty = attractive = lovely

- bloom = flourish

- bones = remains

- beyond the point where land is visible = out of sight of land

- birds in temperate climates = temperate-zone birds

- build = construct

SYNONYMS/C

- located = situated

- consumption = use

- cut = reduce

- cities = urban

- crops = plants which are grown for food

- components = parts

- conscientious = careful

- common = generally

- create = form

- change the direction of = re-route

- cannot be replaced = no substitute for

- complexity = intricacy

- currently = in more recent decades

- categories = types

- create = build

- consistent with = fit

- charging = pricing
- commitment to = engagement
- colleague = peer
- charming = delightful = appealing = enchanting
- chilly = cool
- conditions = factors
- copy = reproduction
- colours = hues
- certain = sure = definite
- capture = seize = arrest
- consulted = asked advice
- collect = accumulate
- contribute to = lead to
- care = concern = protection
- careful = cautious = watchful
- cold = freezing
- comprehend = understand
- confuse = misinterpret

- coincidental = fortuitous

- civil = municipal

- close = shut = fasten

- close = near

- conclude = draw a conclusion

- change = shift

- calm = quiet = tranquil

- complete = finish

- complex = complicated

- cooperation = support and understanding

- construction = building

- city life = urban lifestyles

- complex = complicated = intricate

- competent = capable = qualified

- collect information = establish a databank

- catastrophic = devastating

- compress = condense = squeeze

- concrete = solid

- concur = agree

- conflict = oppose = differ

- consecutive = successive = continuous

- conservative = cautious = restrained

- conscientious = scrupulous = virtuous

- careless = reckless

- conflict = fight = battle = struggle

- cease = stop = discontinue

- courageous = brave

- carefully = meticulously

- channel their feelings = emotional forces in harness

- cemetery = burial ground

- current teaching methods = modern teaching practices

- characteristics = traits

- citizens = residents

- cognitive = perceptual

- cut down on = reduce

- categories = types

- city = metropolitan

- conserving energy = sparing use of energy reserves

- comply with = obey

- cheerful = optimistic

- cheap = worthless

- courageous = brave = heroic

- cowardly = fearful

- contributed to = made a contribution to

- charging = pricing

- contaminate = pollute

- contented = satisfied = pleased

- comparatively = relatively

- come = approach = arrive = reach

- cool = chilly = cold = frosty = frigid

- conform = comply

- conceal = hide

- cozy = comfortable
- congested = overcrowded = stuffed
- continue = persist = persevere
- clarify = explain = simplify
- connect = join = link = attach
- conscious = aware
- courteous = polite
- considerate = thoughtful
- constantly = always = continually
- convenient = handy
- conventional = customary = traditional
- correct = accurate = right
- cry = shout = yell = scream
- cut = chop = reduce
- crazy = insane = mad
- cruel = heartless
- careless = negligent

- chatting on the internet = chatting online

- criminals = people who commit a crime

SYNONYMS/D

- distance = transportation

- disadvantage = drawback

- directly = straight

- decline = downfall

- dull = banal

- dominant = overbearing

- death rate = mortality rate

- domestic = home

- define = distinguish

- dense = tight

- direction = regulation

- difficult situations = challenging activities

- disobey = resist

- discovered = explored

- damage = harm = injure

- divided = split

- dissuade = deter
- disputes = disagreement
- difficulties = challenges
- depart = leave
- disaster = accident
- do not have = lack
- domestic = connected with the home or family
- difficulty in recognizing = hidden or obscured
- drop = discard
- different = unrelated
- discoveries = breakthroughs
- distinctive = different
- dreadful = terrible = unpleasant
- dull = blunt
- depart = leave = exit
- deposit = place
- devised = formulated
- detecting = locating

- dumb = stupid

- documentation = written accounts

- domestic = in homes

- dark = black

- doubt = mistrust

- dawn = sunrise

- dense = thick = heavy = compressed

- due primarily to = mainly because of

- depend (mainly) on = rely (heavily) on

- disclose = eliminate the secrecy

- declined by 50% = halved

- destroy = ruin

- dangerous = hazardous = risky = unsafe

- dark = shadowy = dim = dusky = black

- different = distinct = unlike

- documented evidence = data incidence = scale

- decreasing = decline

- doubt = distrust
- doubtful = vague
- decay = rot = spoil
- delicate = fragile
- disagree = differ = dispute
- dispute = debate = oppose
- demolish = destroy
- delightful = charming = lovely
- dissatisfied = unhappy
- discontinue = stop
- dull = boring = tiring = tiresome = uninteresting = tedious = monotonous
- different = varied
- damage = hurt = impair = harm
- dangerous = unsafe = hazardous
- deduct = subtract
- defend = protect

- detest = dislike = hate

- divide = separate = split

- docile = tame = gentle

- difficult = hard = challenging

- diverse = different = distinct

- dirty = messy

- destroy = demolish

- dishonest = untrustworthy

- dull = uneducated

- destroy = ruin = demolish

- disagreement = contrast = incompatibility

- different functions = various features.

SYNONYMS/E

- estimate = predict

- ecozones = areas where there is a natural community of plants and animals

- encourage = stimulate

- emotions = feelings

- experts = biologists

- enormous = immense

- eyesight = vision

- effect = impact

- economic significance = economic impact

- evidence = clue

- experiments = studies

- evidence = indication

- environmental = ecological

- extremely high = impressive

- each person = each individual

- external = outer

- extended = longer

- efficiently = in the quickest way

- extend = prolonging

- encourage = promote = support = urge

- enemy = opponent = ally

- effective = works well

- effects = consequences

- entirely = wholly

- evident = apparent = obvious = clear

- expenditure on = spent on

- each year = annual

- established = founded = started or created an organization, a system, etc.

- express large numbers = deal with large numbers

- establish targets = setting goals

- enjoy = like

- enlarge = expand = magnify

- earnings = pay = remuneration
- enormous = vast = immense
- early part of the process = early phases of development
- expected = predicted
- expensive = pricey = costly = dear
- exaggerate their claims = overstate their arguments
- examine = analyse
- excited = turbulent
- early = soon = premature
- easy = simple
- evil = bad = wrong = wicked
- excite = arouse = provoke = incite
- exterior = outside = outer
- effortless = easy
- energetic = lively
- end = stop = finish = terminate = conclude = close = halt = cessation
- explain = clarify = define = interpret = justify

SYNONYMS/F

- fertilisers = artificial chemicals added to the land to make crops grow bigger or more quickly

- fresh = new

- fear = be afraid

- false = incorrect

- fast = rapid = quick = swift

- food production = food chain = food supply

- feel = experience

- fix = mend = repair

- fluid = liquid

- fixed = determined

- failed to overcome = made it impossible

- farming = agriculture

- fertile = productive

- free = release

- first = beginning

- first stage = initial stage

- faults = flaws

- features = characteristics

- feelings = emotional responses

- format = pattern

- former = previous = earlier

- fraction = part = portion = segment

- fat = chubby

- fatal = deadly = mortal

- feedback = comments

- frivolous = trivial = unimportant

- full = packed = stuffed

- forbid = prohibit = ban

- forgive = pardon = excuse

- focus on = emphasize

- finish = end

- feasible = possible = attainable = practical

- fabulous = marvelous = amazing

- ferocious = fierce = savage

- fertile = fruitful = productive

- famous = well-known = renowned = famed = eminent.

- fear = fright = dread = scare = panic.

- face = confront = meet

- fair = impartial

- fresh = unused = new

- frigid = freezing = frosty

- furious = angry = enraged = infuriated

- future = tomorrow

- fixed = immobile

- failing = unsuccessful

- filled = occupied

- firm = steady

- false = fake = fraudulent = counterfeit

SYNONYMS/G

- goal = imperative
- grow = rise
- goals = the highest levels of expertise
- grades = results
- generous = giving = big-hearted
- genuine = real = authentic = sincere
- good = nice = fine = well-behaved
- great = outstanding = remarkable
- give their opinions = express their views
- good things = positive things
- give = donate = present = offer
- go around = orbit
- gain = acquire = obtain = receive
- gather = collect = accumulate = compile
- glad = happy = pleased = delighted
- glorious = splendid = magnificent = superb

- gentle = tender = mild

- gratitude = thankfulness = appreciation

- good luck = fortune

- go = move = travel

- good = excellent = fine = wonderful = helpful.

SYNONYMS/H

- have a major impact on = transformed

- halt = call it quits

- happiness = joy

- happen = come about

- have not been diagnosed = undiagnosed

- hard work = effort

- how paper is recycled = the process of paper recycling

- humble = modest

- harsh = strict

- how to produce = the process of producing

- higher corresponds to threefold = three times as much/ triple

- high noise level = loud noise

- help = have a positive effect on

- heat = temperature

- hide = conceal

- happy = content

- humiliate = embarrass

- handy = useful = convenient

- hard = firm = solid

- honest = truthful = sincere = frank

- hospitable = welcoming = gracious

- hostile = aggressive

- huge = vast = immense = great

- hide = conceal

- high = tall

- harsh = rough

- happy = joyful = cheerful = glad = overjoyed = pleased = contented = satisfied = delighted

- **LETTER I**

- infectious diseases = diseases that can pass from one plant to another by the wind or by insects

- in the natural world = throughout nature

- ignore = resist

- intuitive thinking = intuition

- illnesses = ailments

- information = data
- instructed = told
- insufficient = sparse
- illogical = unreasonable
- immoral = unethical
- important = crucial
- incompetent = inept
- intense = extreme
- improve = increase the efficiency of
- increase in population = population growth
- industrial revolution = industrialisation
- immediately = nearly instant
- information = data
- imitate (imitation) = mimic
- impaired = damaged
- innocent = guiltless
- insufficient = inadequate = deficient
- in accordance with = according to

- inaccurate = incorrect

- intelligent = smart = bright

- increasing = soaring

- interior access = inner staircases

- initiate = bring about

- interesting = provocative = engrossing

- identify the problem = understand the problem

- isolated = inaccessible

- internal = inner = inside

- in excess of = over

- increase = expand = rise

- irrelevant = inappropriate = unrelated

- irritate = annoy

- introduction = invention

- identical = alike = duplicate

- inactive = lazy

- ignore = disregard

- important = vital = indispensable

- interesting = fascinating = engaging = attractive = intriguing = captivating = enchanting

- impossible = unachievable

- infants = very young children

- intriguing = fascinating

- in essence = essentially

- independent = self-reliant

- inappropriate = unsuitable

- increase = enlarge = amplify

- ingenious = clever = creative

- impetuous = impulsive = reckless

- important = significant = meaningful

- inappropriate = unsuitable = wrong

- ignorant = unaware

- immaculate = spotless = pure

- imperfect = defective = faulty

- imperative = compulsory = mandatory

- involved with = associated with

- idle = inactive

- immature = childish = inexperienced

- impolite = rude

- indefinite = unclear

- insignificant = unimportant

- immune = resistant

- impartial = neutral = unbiased = fair

- idea = thought = concept

- incident = event

- incompatible characteristics = paradox

SYNONYMS/K

- keep = save = protect = guard

- kind = considerate = tender = thoughtful

- kind = wonderful

- knowledgeable = smart

SYNONYMS/L

- launched = initiated

- lived apart = be separated at birth

- large = big = massive = huge

- last = final = end

- look like = resemble

- levels = storeys

- lethargic = tired

- lifted = raised

- leave out = omit

- life expectancy = lifetime

- lower secondary schools = middle-years education

- least = fewest = minimum = smallest

- lacking = insufficient

- long-term = sustainable

- liable to = can happen

- less time spent on exercises = shorten the practice

- learn = acquire

- long = lengthy

- lure = attract = seduce

- long-lost traits = ancestral features

- left = soared out of

- limit = minimize

- limited = incomplete

- local people = communities

- large city = megalopolis

- long-term = lasting/extending over a long time

- little doubt = almost certainly

- luxurious = extravagant = elegant

- lack = deficit

- love = like = fancy = cherish = adore = treasure = appreciate

- levels of unemployment = unemployment rate

SYNONYMS/M

- motifs = patterns = images

- material = commodity

- magnify = expand = enlarge = exaggerate

- misfortune = hardship

- mathematical method = statistical concept

- moved = relocation

- most people = almost every individual

- manager = boss

- mass production = print out huge numbers

- mainly = most important

- mishandling = bungling

- make payment = pay for

- movement = transport

- mean = unkind = malicious = nasty

- mend = repair = fix

- motorised vehicles = buses and trucks

- more than = exceed
- make the noise stop = turn the noise off
- moulded = reshaped
- man-made = synthetic
- mild = moderate
- moral = ethical = virtuous = righteous
- mature = adult
- most = maximum
- maximum = greatest
- minimum = least
- mobile = moveable
- monotonous = boring = tedious
- mysterious = secret
- manufactured = produced
- move onto = pass onto
- most of = nearly all of
- moves = gestures
- more = increased

- modified = qualified

- migrate back = return

- medical technique = treatment

- mean = cruel = inconsiderate

- movable = portable

- manufacture = produce

SYNONYMS/N

- need = require

- non-fossil-based fuels = renewable energy

- needed = required

- nature = essence

- not traditional = new

- natural forests = primary forests

- not limit = transcend

- neat = clean, tidy, well-organized.

- new = fresh = original = current

- noisy = rowdy

- noise = disturbance

- normal = ordinary = typical, usual

- negligent = careless = inattentive

- naughty = bad = disobedient

- neat = clean = orderly = tidy

- neglectful = careless

- no limit = never reach maximum

- not charged = not have to pay

- new = recent

- nervous energy = psychic tension

- new technologies = modern technologies

- not natural = artificial

- not appreciated = undervalued

- now = current

- need = requirement

SYNONYMS/O

- observe = see

- omit = strip out = leave out

- ordinary = conventional

- over the counter = in the shops

- officials = authorities

- overcome = deal with

- open = begin

- occur frequently = are common

- only = solely

- overdirect = too much guidance

- overcome shyness = learn to be more outgoing

- one explanation = another possibility

- ordinary = commonplace

- old = antique

- obsolete = dated = antiquated

- optimistic = hopeful = confident

- odours = smell

- overcome = getting rid of

- occur more than once = repeated

- outgoing = assured

- obey = comply

- old people = people who are retired

- offend = displease = disgust

- outstanding = extraordinary

- odd = weird = strange

- obey = comply

SYNONYMS/P

- plant = grow

- place = locate

- paintings = works

- precious metals = gold, silver

- premature = early

- pretty = lovely = beautiful = attractive

- pleasing = appealing

- perform = carry out

- pioneered = first suggested

- persuasive = powerful

- play it safe = avoid risk

- personality = character

- potential = possibilities

- promptly = immediately

- profit = gain = earnings = benefit

- prohibit = forbid = restrict

- policy initiative = strategy

- previous events = past experience

- plants = stations

- provide a view of = overlook

- private transport = car

- principles = laws

- put together = assembled

- place = deposit

- prompt = punctual = timely

- prosperous = thriving = successful = flourishing

- prevent = prohibit = hinder

- permit = allow

- prior to = beforehand

- pictures = images

- problem = difficulty

- permit = allow

- promotion = advancement

- prominent = distinguished = eminent

- personal values = individual properties
- pessimistic view = seems to be getting worse
- prevail upon = have influence in = persuade
- principles = essential features
- publicity = press
- program cost = program fee
- physical changes = hormonal changes
- processes = stages
- perfect = flawless
- precious = valuable
- plausible = believable = reasonable = logical
- polite = gracious = courteous
- place = area = plot = region = location = situation
- proportion = percentage = rate
- poverty rate = level of poverty = poverty level = the percentage of people who live in poverty
- production = manufacture = be produced = be made = be manufactured
- per person = per capita

- people who use cars = car users = car commuters = people who commute by car = people who travel by car

- people who cycle to work = cycling commuters

- public = individuals

- produce accurate work = make fewer errors

- problems = difficulties

- present beliefs = contemporary perceptions

- picked out = chose

- pesticides = potent chemicals

- pagoda = temple building

- prehistoric = ancient

- patience = perseverance

- permanent = enduring = lasting

- prevent misunderstanding = resolve any confusion

- peace = harmony

- persuade = convince = influence

- peace = quiet

- preceding = previous

SYNONYMS/Q

- quickly = rapidly

- question = interrogate = inquire = ask

- quiet = silent = tranquil

- quick = speedy

- quit = cease = stop = withdraw

SYNONYMS/R

- rely on = be dependent on

- rules = laws

- restrict = curb

- really successful = achieve at a higher level

- rainfall = precipitation

- rotate = turn

- recording of events = documentation of history

- replication = reproducing

- regarded as =considered

- researchers with differing attitudes = sceptics and advocates

- remove = extract

- react = respond

- reason = caused

- remedy = repair

- rude = unfriendly

- replaced = upgrade

- rational thinking = judgment

- reversible = run backwards

- responsibility = moral obligation

- reticence = shyness

- remains = fragments

- re-emerge = reappear

- respond = reply

- resemble = look like

- regular = continual

- referring to = talk about

- response = reply

- run their own business = open their own business/ company

- regulations = standards

- relies on = draw on

- reliable = predictable

- relationships with other people = social experience

- reflection = movements in the mirror

- reveal = tell

- recognize = distinguish

- remember = recall

- retain = learn

- raise = lift

- recognize = certify = admit officially (usually in writing)

- restricted = limited

- recognise the difference = distinguish

- rise = growing = increased

- release = punctured

- recommence = continue

- real = authentic

- reluctant = unwilling = hesitant

- remote = secluded = isolated = distant

- rarely = seldom

- reduce = shrink

- remarkable = outstanding

- rough = harsh

- release = discharge

- rude = discourteous

- rich = wealthy

- risky = hazardous

- reputable = honorable

- resist = oppose = withstand

- recreation = amusement = pleasure

- reduce = lessen = decrease = diminish

- reliable = trustworthy

- reveal = show = disclose

- ridiculous = nonsensical = foolish

- remove = eliminate = get rid of

SYNONYMS/S

- shut out water = seal off from water

- sea = ocean

- support = back up

- satisfying = rewarding

- suffers = experiences

- supplementary = extra

- silence = absence of a sound

- shade = shelter from the heat

- steps = measures

- strengthen = deepen

- share = interchange

- socially disadvantaged = deprived

- self-reliance = independence

- support = backup

- significance = importance

- show statistically = provide precise, valid or reliable data

- seem to contradict = sound paradoxical
- significant = important
- several times = on more than one occasion
- signals = radio waves
- site = station
- seeking = looking for
- searching for = looking for
- stop = quit = cease = terminate
- strenuous = vigorous = laborious
- suitable = appropriate
- small = minor
- stop = halt
- sea life = fish and other creatures
- saw the importance = understood the need
- success rate = hit-rate
- surprising = unexpectedly
- similar to = not unusual
- severe weather conditions = typhoons

- stop = constrain

- send = deliver

- stop = close down = put a halt to = bring a halt to

- separate from = independent of

- staff = employees

- sleep disorders = sleep disturbance

- shy = timid

- separate = disconnect

- sparse = empty

- stable = steady = unchanging

- stimulate = motivate

- same = similar

- sharp = bright

- strict = severe

- strong = powerful = mighty

- stupid = dense = foolish

- smart = intelligent = clever

- sadness = depression
- scatter = disperse
- show = present = reveal = demonstrate = display = exhibit
- slow = gradual = leisurely
- selfish = stingy
- sad = unhappy
- subsequent = following = succeeding
- small = tiny
- sensible = rational
- separate = disconnect = detach
- small = little
- swift = fast = speedy = hasty
- synthetic = man-made = artificial
- sloppy = disorderly
- sick = ill
- slim = slender = thin
- small = little
- sociable = friendly

- successful = thriving = prosperous = triumphant

- surplus = excess = additional = extra

- strange = odd = weird, outlandish, curious, unique, exclusive, irregular

- sales = turnover = how much money is made = income = revenue

- spending = expenditure

- sort = classify

- start a business = own a business/ company

- shopping on the internet = online shopping = buying/purchasing online

- sales of fast food = turnover from fast food

SYNONYMS/T

- taken out = removed

- the folklore = the local belief

- the most important step = key step

- time limit = deadline

- trend of the period = fashion of the time

- tradesmen = merchants

- the rapid growth = the spectacular growth

- transport methods = transport modes

- technological developments = information technologies

- take gambles = take chances

- techniques = methods = practices

- transport mode = means of transport

- test = examination

- test = experiment

- to investigate = to analyse

- the most important = major

- to give up = to abandon

- 2 decades = 20 years

- the most vividly coloured red = the reddest

- took = carried

- tools = facilities

- the question = the puzzle

- transmission = pass along communication channels

- transmitted = sent back

- transmit = sent out

- thin = skinny

- tragic = sorrowful

- take = receive

- terrible = awful = bad

- threat = endangered

- today = current

- today = now

- teaching activities = methods

- three different types = three separate ways

- to copy = to replicate = to reproduce

- the world economy = the global economy

- to be sure = to ensure

- to proceed = to continue

- total = whole = entire = complete

- tell = inform = notify

- take = pick = choose = select

- the level of income = the rate of income = the income rate = the income level = the level of revenue = the revenue rate = the revenue level

- the elderly = elderly people = senior citizens

- the amount of time spent = the time spent

- the majority of people = most of the people = most people

- transport = deliver = carry

- to rise = to increase = to grow = to go up

- to decrease = to fall = to reduce = to go down = to drop = to decline

SYNONYMS/U

- uncover = reveal

- underestimate = overlook

- universal = just about everybody

- unjust = unfair

- unemployment = out of work

- unlike = a fundamental difference

- unpredictably = erratically

- understand = recognize

- upset = find painful, distressing

- unnecessary = superfluous = redundant

- unpleasant = offensive

- uncommon = unusual

- unknown = not renowned

- unwanted material = waste

- upgrade = improve

- unsuccessful = fruitless

- unfit = unsuited

- unexpectedly = without warning = unpredictable

- unusual = exceptional

- uncertain = unsure

- unbiased = impartial = unprejudiced = fair

- unite = join

- unaware = unconscious

- unnecessary = optional

- unimportant = meaningless

- untruthful = insincere

- uninteresting = dull

- usual = ordinary

- unpleasant = unacceptable

SYNONYMS/V

- view = vision

- valuable = precious

- views = convictions

- views = attitudes

- vibrate = shake

- vacant = unoccupied = empty

- vague = unclear = indistinct = obscure

- vague = ambiguous

SYNONYMS/W

- world = international

- working together = coordination

- worldwide = international

- wider = greater

- water consumption = the amount of water consumed

- ways of learning = techniques for learning = approaches to learning

- waste = trash = rubbish

- well known = famous

- wholehearted = sincere

- wise = knowing = smart

- water is pumped = pumped with the water

- wild = stubborn

- weak = frail

- work = labor

- wasteful = extravagant

- wealth = prosperity = assets

- weary = tired = fatigued = lethargic

- wonderful = incredible = splendid = marvelous

- waste output = the amounts of waste

- work for an employer = work for other people

- wrong = incorrect

- waste paper = paper that has been thrown away

- works of art = pieces

CONCLUSION

Thank you again for downloading this book on *"IELTS Reading Strategies: The Ultimate Guide with Tips and Tricks on How to Get a Target Band Score of 8.0+ in 10 Minutes a Day."* and reading all the way to the end. I'm extremely grateful.

If you know of anyone else who may benefit from the useful strategies, structures, tips, guides for IELTS reading that are revealed in this book, please help me inform them of this book. I would greatly appreciate it.

Finally, if you enjoyed this book and feel that it has added value to your work and study in any way, please take a couple of minutes to share your thoughts and post a REVIEW on Amazon. Your feedback will help me to continue to write other books of IELTS topic that helps you get the best results. Furthermore, if you write a simple REVIEW with positive words for this book on Amazon, you can help hundreds or perhaps thousands of other readers who may want to improve their English reading skill sounding like a native speaker. Like you, they worked hard for every penny they spend on books. With the information and recommendation you provide, they would be more likely to take action right away. We really look forward to reading your review.

Thanks again for your support and good luck!

If you enjoy my book, please write a POSITIVE REVIEW on Amazon.

-- Rachel Mitchell --

CHECK OUT OTHER BOOKS

Go here to check out other related books that might interest you:

IELTS Listening Strategies: The Ultimate Guide with Tips, Tricks and Practice on How to Get a Target Band Score of 8.0+ in 10 Minutes a Day.

https://www.amazon.com/dp/B07845S1MG

Ielts Writing Task 2 Samples : Over 450 High-Quality Model Essays for Your Reference to Gain a High Band Score 8.0+ In 1 Week (Box set) https://www.amazon.com/dp/B077BYQLPG

Ielts Academic Writing Task 1 Samples: Over 450 High Quality Samples for Your Reference to Gain a High Band Score 8.0+ In 1 Week (Box set) https://www.amazon.com/dp/B077CC5ZG4

Shortcut To English Collocations: Master 2000+ English Collocations In Used Explained Under 20 Minutes A Day (5 books in 1 Box set)

https://www.amazon.com/dp/B06W2P6S22

IELTS Writing Task 1 + 2: The Ultimate Guide with Practice to Get a Target Band Score of 8.0+ In 10 Minutes a Day

https://www.amazon.com/dp/B075DFYPG6

IELTS Speaking Strategies: The Ultimate Guide With Tips, Tricks, And Practice On How To Get A Target Band Score Of 8.0+ In 10 Minutes A Day.

https://www.amazon.com/dp/B075JCW65G

Shortcut To Ielts Writing: The Ultimate Guide To Immediately Increase Your Ielts Writing Scores.

https://www.amazon.com/dp/B01JV7EQGG

Common English Mistakes Explained With Examples: Over 600 Mistakes Almost Students Make and How to Avoid Them in Less Than 5 Minutes A Day

https://www.amazon.com/dp/B072PXVHNZ

Paraphrasing Strategies: 10 Simple Techniques For Effective Paraphrasing In 5 Minutes Or Less

https://www.amazon.com/dp/B071DFG27Q

Legal Vocabulary In Use: Master 600+ Essential Legal Terms And Phrases Explained In 10 Minutes A Day

http://www.amazon.com/dp/B01L0FKXPU

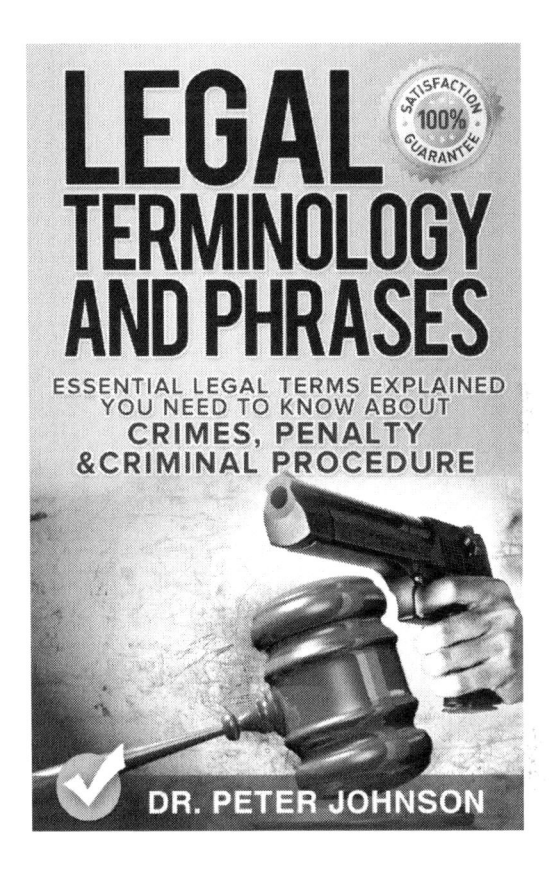

Legal Terminology And Phrases: Essential Legal Terms Explained You Need To Know About Crimes, Penalty And Criminal Procedure

http://www.amazon.com/dp/B01L5EB54Y

Productivity Secrets For Students: The Ultimate Guide To Improve Your Mental Concentration, Kill Procrastination, Boost Memory And Maximize Productivity In Study

http://www.amazon.com/dp/B01JS52UT6

Daughter of Strife: 7 Techniques On How To Win Back Your Stubborn Teenage Daughter

https://www.amazon.com/dp/B01HS5E3V6

Parenting Teens With Love And Logic: A Survival Guide To Overcoming The Barriers Of Adolescence About Dating, Sex And Substance Abuse

https://www.amazon.com/dp/B01JQUTNPM

http://www.amazon.com/dp/B01K0ARNA4

Printed in Great Britain
by Amazon